Wings

A DRAMA

By Arthur Kopit

S A M U E L   F R E N C H ,   I N C .

25 WEST 45TH STREET   NEW YORK 10036

7623 SUNSET BOULEVARD   HOLLYWOOD 90046

LONDON   TORONTO

To George Kopit, my father
1913–1977

CAST

EMILY STILSON .... *Constance Cummings*

AMY .... *Mary-Joan Negro*

DOCTORS .... *Roy Steinberg, Ross Petty*

NURSES .... *Gina Franz, Mary Michelle Rutherfurd*

BILLY .... *James Tolkan*

MR. BROWNSTEIN .... *Carl Don*

MRS. TIMMINS .... *Betty Pelzer*

WINGS was given its first stage performance at the Yale Repertory Theatre in New Haven, Connecticut, on March 3, 1978, with the following cast:

EMILY STILSON .... *Constance Cummings*

AMY .... *Marianne Owen*

DOCTORS .... *Geoffrey Pierson, Roy Steinberg*

NURSES .... *Caris Corfman, Carol Ostrow*

BILLY .... *Richard Grusin*

MR. BROWNSTEIN .... *Ira Bernstein*

MRS. TIMMINS .... *Betty Pelzer*

Directed by JOHN MADDEN
Designed by ANDREW JACKNESS
Costumes by JEANNE BUTTON
Lighting by TOM SCHRAEDER
Sound by TOM VOEGELI
Music by HERB PILHOFER

LYCEUM THEATRE

Ⓢ A Shubert Organization Theatre

Gerald Schoenfeld, *Chairman*   Bernard B. Jacobs, *President*

THE KENNEDY CENTER presents
in association with CLAUS VON BULOW

CONSTANCE CUMMINGS

in

WINGS

by

ARTHUR KOPIT

with

MARY-JOAN NEGRO

Carl Don   **Gina Franz**   **Betty Pelzer**

Ross Petty   **Mary Michelle Rutherfurd**

Roy Steinberg   **James Tolkan**

Scenery by   *Costumes by*   *Lighting by*   *Sound by*
Andrew Jackness **Jeanne Button** **Tom Schraeder** **Tom Voegeli**

Directed by

JOHN MADDEN

Produced for the Kennedy Center by Roger L. Stevens

"Wings" was originally produced on the stage by the Yale Repertory Theatre,
New Haven, Connecticut.

The Producers and Theatre Management are Members
of The League of New York Theatres and Producers, Inc.

SOUND TAPES

Please be advised that Samuel French, Inc. can furnish a set of Sound Tapes, for a period of 8 weeks, upon receipt of the following:

1. Name & address of organization.
2. Exact dates of performance.
3. Deposit of $25.00, which is refundable, upon the safe return of the tape immediately following the production.
4. Music Royalty of $15.00 for the first performance and $10.00 for each additional performance.
5. Mailing charge of $2.00 for first class mail.

All monies must be paid in advance of shipment. Tapes must be returned immediately following production. Please allow at least a week for shipment.

PREFACE

In the fall of 1976, I was commissioned to write an original radio play for Earplay, the drama project of National Public Radio. They did not stipulate what the play should be about, only that it should not last longer than an hour. *Wings* was the result. It has since, of course, been altered and expanded, mainly to accommodate the visual components of my central character's condition. But the play was, and still remains, essentially about language disorder and its implications. For that reason, radio was the perfect initial medium; it did not permit me to get lost in the myriad and always fascinating perceptual aberrations that can accompany any severe damage to the brain. I now believe that if I had conceived *Wings* directly for the stage instead, I would have inevitably found myself seduced by the stage's greater freedom into investigating at length these astonishing but ultimately peripheral aspects of aphasia. Most likely, more characters would have been introduced, a welter of extraordinary syndromes revealed and examined. If brain damage is terrifying to behold, it is also alluring. One feels the need to avert one's eyes and hide, and the equal if not greater need to keep looking. It is a very scary business, this job of exploring who we are. Very quickly, I suspect, my focus would have vanished. All of which is to say that if *Wings* exhibits in its present form any excellence of vision and craft, that excellence is without question a direct function of the rigor imposed on it by its initial incarnation. For that reason, I must express a deep debt of gratitude to Earplay for having commissioned this play, and particularly to the man who directed both its initial version and its first production on the stage at Yale, John Madden.

There is a question which I suspect must arise inevitably in the mind of anyone who reads or sees this play: to what degree is *Wings* faithful to fact, to what degree sheer speculation.

In the spring of 1976, seven months before Earplay was to commission me to write on a subject of my choosing, my father suffered a major stroke which rendered him incapable of speech. Furthermore, because of certain other complications, all related to his aphasia, and all typical of stroke, it was impossible to know how much he comprehended. Certainly there was no doubt that his capacity to comprehend had been drastically impaired and reduced. As best I could, I tried to understand what he was going through. It seemed to me that, regardless of how reduced his senses were, the isolation he was being forced to endure had to verge on the intolerable; clearly, he had not lost all comprehension—the look of terror in his eyes was unmistakable. Yet, not only did he tolerate this state; every now and then, if one watched carefully enough, something escaped from this shell that was his body and his prison, something almost but not quite palpable, something not readily brought to the attention of a nurse (I tried it once but she saw nothing), something which I felt possessed a kind of glow or flicker, rather like a lamp way off in the dark, something only barely perceptible. I took these faint flashes to be him signaling. And although I allowed for the possibility that what I was perceiving was nothing but mirage, or the mirrored reflections of my own hopeful and constant signalings to him, nonetheless, it seemed to me (indeed, seemed irrefutable) that in some ineffably essential way, reduced as he was, he was still the same person he had been. This thought was both heartening and frightful. To what extent was he still intact? To what extent was he aware of what had befallen him? *What was it like inside?*

And then Earplay came along. By its very nature, radio seemed to offer an especially appropriate means of exploring these particular questions.

I recognized at once that I could not deal directly with my father. For one thing, I was too close to him to hold any hope of objectivity. For another, his case was too severe, too grim, my audience would turn away. So I looked else-where for a model. The questions would remain the same, of course, and just as valid; my understanding of my father's world would have to come—if indeed it could at all—through analogy. I decided to focus on two patients I had met at the Burke Rehabilitation Center in White Plains, New York, where my father had been transferred after his stay in the hospital. Both were women: one was old, in her late seventies, perhaps older; the other, not quite thirty. Like my father, both had suffered major strokes, though neither was as incapacitated as he; both at least could talk. Certainly they could not talk well.

The speech of the younger woman was fluent and pos-sessed normal intonations, cadence, and syntactical structure—in fact, to such an extent that anyone who did not understand English would have sworn she was making sense. Nonetheless, her sentences were laced with a kind of babbled jargon so that, by and large, she made no sense at all. In her early stages, she seemed unaware of this appal-ling deficit.* In contrast, the older woman's words had no fluency, no melodic inflection, no syntactical richness. Her words emerged with difficulty and sounded like something composed for a telegram. Modifiers and conjunctions for the most part were absent. But at least her words made sense. The problem was, as often as not, the sense they conveyed was not the sense she intended. Though she usu-ally was aware of these "mistakes," or at least could be made aware of them, she could not prevent them from oc-curring. Neither could she readily correct them. Aside from her aphasia, each woman was relatively free of other symptoms.

---

* This particular kind of speech, typical of a certain form of aphasia, is characterized by neologisms, and sounds very much like double talk or gibberish. The word *gibberish*, however, suggests psychosis and dementia, and is therefore inappropriate for describing an effect of organic brain disease; the term *jargonaphasia* is used instead.

I had met the older woman while accompanying my father one afternoon on his rounds. When he went down for speech therapy, she was one of the three other patients in the room. I had never observed a speech therapy session before and was nervous. The day, I recall vividly, was warm, humid. The windows of the room were open. A scent of flowers suffused the air. To get the session started, the therapist asked the older woman if she could name the seasons of the year. With much effort, she did, though not in proper order. She seemed annoyed with herself for having any difficulty at all with such a task. The therapist then asked her which of these seasons corresponded to the present. The woman turned at once to the window. She could see the garden, the flowers. Her eyes were clear, alert; there was no question but that she understood what was wanted. I cannot remember having ever witnessed such an intense struggle. At first, she did nothing but sit calmly and wait for the word to arrive on its own. When it didn't, she tried to force the word out by herself, through thinking; as if to assist what clearly was a process of expulsion, she scrunched her face up, squeezed her eyelids shut. But no word emerged. Physically drained, her face drenched with sweat, she tried another trick: she cocked her head and listened to the birds, whose sound was incessant. When this too led to nothing, she sniffed the air. When nothing came of this strategy either, she turned her attention to what she was wearing, a light cotton dress; she even touched the fabric. Finally, something connected. Her lips began to form a word. She shut her eyes. Waited. The word emerged. *Winter*.

When informed that it was summer she seemed astonished, how was it possible? . . . a mistake like that . . . obviously she knew what season it was, anyone with eyes could tell at once what season it was! . . . and yet . . . She looked over at where I sat and shook her head in dismay, then laughed and said, "This is really nuts, isn't it!"

I sat there, stunned. I could not believe that anyone making a mistake of such gross proportions and with such catastrophic implications could laugh at it.

So there would be no misunderstanding, the therapist quickly pointed out that this mistake stemmed completely from her stroke; in no way was she demented. The woman smiled (she knew all that) and turned away, stared back out the window at the garden. *This is really nuts, isn't it!*—I could not get her phrase from my mind. In its intonation, it had conveyed no feeling of anger, resignation, or despair. Rather, it had conveyed amazement, and in that amazement, a trace (incredible as it seemed) of delight. This is not to suggest that anyone witnessing this incident could, even for an instant, have imagined that she was in any sense pleased with her condition. The amazement, and its concomitant delight, seemed to me to reflect only an acknowledgment that her condition was extraordinary, and in no way denied or obviated the terror or the horror that were at its core. By some (I supposed) nourishing spring of inner strength and light, of whose source I had no idea, she had come to a station in her life from which she could perceive in what was happening something that bore the aspect of adventure, and it was through this perhaps innate capacity to perceive and appreciate adventure, and perhaps in this sense only, that she found some remaining modicum of delight, which I suspect kept her going. Of course, all this was speculation. As I said, I was stunned. The therapist asked her to try again and she did. And she got it—summer! With great excitement, she tried once again. Same result. She had it! Summer! She tried again. *Winter*. It was lost. She heard but could do nothing. She shook her head in consternation. Smiled in wonderment. In the course of the session, I discovered we shared the same birthday.

Later that afternoon, I inquired as to who she was, and was told she was a former aviatrix and wing-walker. I believe my response to this news was *"What?"*—although I think I may have said, *"Wing-walker?"* Either way, my composure was slipping. I felt decidedly inadequate.

A nurse brought me to her room (she was out, gone down to dinner) and showed me a photograph pinned up on her wall; it had been taken when she was in her twenties. In the photograph, a biplane sits on a large grassy field, a crowded grandstand in the distance, its front railing draped with flags. The plane is a Curtiss Jenny. A pilot sits in the rearmost of its two open cockpits; she is standing out on its lower wing, white silk scarf around her neck, goggles set back on top of her leather helmet. She wears jodhpurs, boots, a leather jacket. Her face is lean and handsome and imperious. The same noble and slightly quizzical smile I'd seen that afternoon is there. Her right hand is holding on to the wire stays behind her. The propeller is spinning; apparently, her plane is about to take off. Several nurses come in and join us in staring at the photograph. Her eyes seem on fire; they are filled with an unquenchable eager passion. Her left hand is waving toward the camera and the unseen throng.

Needless to say, had I invented her, the invention would have been excessive, would have strained credulity—only in dreams and fiction did one meet persons such as this. Yet, here she was, she existed. Everyone at Burke who knew her agreed that the fortitude and *esprit* I'd seen that afternoon in the therapy session were no aberration. By nature she was one of the bravest, most extraordinary persons they had ever met. There was no other choice: she was my model.

With that decision, a task that might otherwise have been little more than grim took on the aspects of an adventure. As scrupulously as possible, I would try to explore, through her mind, this terrible and awesome realm of being. Surely, that realm bore resemblance to my father's. Courage was not her quality alone.

The title came at once. Also, with it, two recognitions: if *Wings* was to be effective, it would have to deal specifically with its central character and not with some general condition called stroke; at the same time, to be effective, it would have to possess an absolutely solid clinical accuracy.

To these ends, I began an exhaustive study of airplanes and brain damage—unquestionably a weird conjunction of subjects. The study of airplanes was simple. Libraries provided everything I had to know about early aviation—how the old biplanes were flown, who flew them, what their cockpits looked like, felt like; and especially about that remarkable post-World War I phenomenon known as barnstorming, when pilots (many of them women) toured the country, thrilling crowds with exhibitions of their marvelous, death-defying daring and skill. Burke was where I went to study brain damage and rehabilitation.

It quickly became clear that, for my purposes at least, the speech patterns of this older woman (due to the nature of her stroke) were not as varied and therefore not as interesting as the speech patterns of many other patients.

For greater linguistic richness, I turned to the patient in her late twenties as the principal model for my central character's speech. In her own right, this young woman was as exceptional as the older. Certainly she was no less brave. When I met her, she was able to acknowledge the gravity of her condition, and fought all tendencies to self-pity and despair. With as much cheerfulness as she could muster (her capacity for hope seemed limitless), she worked every moment that she could at the one task in her life that mattered: the reassembling of her shattered world. But there was yet another exceptional aspect to this young woman, and in truth it was this that made me turn to her as the model not only for my central character's patterns of speech but, in fact, ultimately, her very processes of thought: *she was left-handed*. From this one seemingly insignificant trait, many remarkable abilities derived.

In a right-handed person, the left hemisphere of the cerebral cortex is dominant and controls all activities connected with speech and analytic consciousness. However, for persons who are by nature left-handed, some of the left hemisphere's usual functions are taken over by the normally nonverbal and intuitive right. Should such a person suffer a stroke or injury to the left cerebral hemisphere, he stands a good chance of retaining a degree of verbal lucidity and insight inaccessible to those whose left hemisphere maintains sole dominance. This was the case with the young woman I met at Burke. Because of her left-handedness, she possessed the rare ability to recognize and articulate, to a slight but still significant extent, her own patterns of thought. Repeatedly, she would describe a certain dividedness within her head, as if she literally sensed the separate hemispheres at work, usually in contradiction to each other. In such instances, she would actually refer to her mind's "two sides," and frequently accompany this description with a slicing gesture of her hand, clearly suggestive of a vertically symmetrical division of her entire body. Once, she described coming to a large puddle. With great amusement she recounted how one side of her head told her to go left, while the other side told her to go right; to end the controversy and resolve the debate, she walked through the middle.

At Burke I studied her attempts at keeping a journal, listened to hours of taped interviews between her and her speech therapist, and of course, as often as possible, talked directly to her myself. She seemed to understand something of my project and its purposes, and seemed pleased that somehow she could be of help. Gradually, an image of a remarkable and quite vivid interior landscape began to form in my mind, frightening and awesome in its details, its blatant gaps, its implications.

But there was still another person crucial to my research: her therapist, Jacqueline Doolittle. Her knowledge of aphasia was my touchstone. At all hours of the day and sometimes night, I would call Mrs. Doolittle with some generally naïve question about the brain, and she, with limitless good humor, would set me straight. It is both astonishing and humbling the number of assumptions one can make in this field which are absolutely wrong. Nonetheless, I kept phoning and, if not phoning, stopping by her office, usually unannounced. To her credit, and perhaps to mine, she never threw me out. Gradually, things became clearer. I should point out, Mrs. Doolittle's understanding of aphasia went far beyond the clinical: Jacqueline Doolittle had herself been aphasic once.

Her aphasia had resulted from a head injury sustained in an auto accident. Eventually she recovered, and her recollections of this period are like visions of a sojourn in another realm: vivid and detailed. Without a doubt, it was this experience that lay at the root of her exceptional empathic abilities as a therapist.

What she described was a world of fragments, a world without dimension, a world where time meant nothing constant, and from which there seemed no method of escape. She thought she had either gone mad or been captured by an unknown enemy for purposes she could not fathom, and in fact took the hospital she was in to be a farmhouse in disguise, controlled by her captors. For a long time, she was unable to distinguish that the words she spoke were jargon, and wondered why everyone she saw spoke to her in a foreign tongue. Her state was one of utter isolation, confusion, terror, and disarray. She wondered if perhaps she was dreaming. Sometimes the thought occurred to her that she was dead. Then, very gradually, the swelling in her head subsided, and little by little the cells in her left cerebral hemisphere began to make their proper neural connections. She began to understand what people said. When she spoke, the right words, as if by magic, started flowing. She returned to the world she knew. *Wings* owes much of its structure and detail to these recollections.

How much of this play, then, is speculation?

Wings is a play about a woman whom I have called Emily Stilson. Though she suffers a stroke, in no way is it a case study, and in its execution I have assiduously avoided any kind of clinical or documentary approach. Indeed, it has been so conceived and constructed that its audience can, for the most part, observe this realm that she is in only through her own consciousness. In short, *Wings* is a work of speculation informed by fact.

But any attempt to render a person's consciousness through words, even autobiography, must be speculative. Where thoughts are concerned, there are no infallible reporters. What we remember of our pasts is filtered by our sensibilities and predilections, and can as easily be imaginary as real. To what extent did Jacqui Doolittle remember only what she wanted to? To what extent did her mind, in its damaged state, withhold from her consciousness something essential to her experience? Given that she was suffering a severe language deficit, how much can we trust her verbal recollections? In this arena, hard facts do not exist. Yet, if we cannot hope for what is provable, we at least can strive for what is plausible. By any criteria, Jacqui Doolittle's account has emotional validity. The same holds true for the young left-handed woman's. It was this emotional truth, informed by fact, that I was after. So far as I was able, I have avoided in this play any colorations of my own and, as far as I know, have attributed to Emily Stilson no symptoms that are unlikely or impossible. Though Emily Stilson is a composite of many persons, and derives finally from my imagination, I have worked as if in fact she existed, and in this light, and within the limitations of this form, have felt myself obliged to render her condition as it was, not as I might have preferred it.

There are two books whose influence on me I would like to acknowledge, and which I strongly recommend to anyone interested in further explorations of this subject: Howard Gardner's *The Shattered Mind,* and A. R. Luria's *The Man with a Shattered World.*

I would also like to acknowledge the crucial role of Robert Brustein, as Dean of the Yale School of Drama, in the evolution of this play. Mr. Brustein had heard the radio play performed, and had expressed his admiration of the work. In November of 1977, he called me to say that he had been thinking about the play, and had come to believe it could be even more effective on the stage. A slot had opened in the Yale Rep's spring schedule. Was I interested?

Not only was I interested, I was flabbergasted. Since summer, when I had first heard *Wings* performed, I had been trying to figure out if it was possible to adapt it to the stage. The problems, it turned out, were considerable, both structurally and thematically. That afternoon, indeed less than an hour before the call came in, I had suddenly realized how to do it.

For those who may have missed the issue, *Forbes Magazine* ranks playwrighting extremely low on the list of Easy Ways to Earn One's Fortune. In fact, it is no simple matter to earn one's living at its practice. I would therefore like to express both my family's and my deep gratitude to the Rockefeller Foundation for a generous and timely grant, which alone enabled me to devote, with ease of mind, the enormous time and energy that I soon found the work demanded, both in the writing and in the research.

For their extensive and always generous assistance in that research, I am profoundly indebted and grateful to the Burke Rehabilitation Center; and especially to Jacqueline Doolittle.

A.L.K.

I weave in and out of the strange clouds, hidden in my tiny cockpit, submerged, alone, on the magnitude of this weird, unhuman space, venturing where man has never been, perhaps never meant to go. Am I myself a living, breathing, earth-bound body, or is this a dream of death I'm passing through? Am I alive, or am I really dead, a spirit in a spirit world. Am I actually in a plane, or have I crashed on some wordly mountain, and is this the afterlife?

Charles Lindbergh, *The Spirit of St. Louis*.

NOTES ON OTHER PRODUCTIONS OF *WINGS*

I cannot emphasize strongly enough how crucial it is that anyone directing WINGS do some homework first. The production must be grounded in a thorough clinical authenticity. This is not that hard to come by. Several books will help, and are a good preliminary step. *The Shattered Mind* by Howard Gardner is a first-rate introduction to the brain and brain damage; A. R. Luria's "The Man with a Shattered World" is another fine and very helpful book, though the damage suffered by the man in Luria's study differs significantly in his symptoms from anyone in WINGS. Still, the Luria book communicates an extraordinary sense of what the world is like for someone whose mind has been drastically and permanently altered, and it cannot help but prove useful to a director of WINGS.

I also strongly suggest that the director, designer, and cast visit a first-rate rehabilitation center. It is vital, particularly for the director, that there be real-life models to draw upon. I don't think, for example, that the group therapy scene can work unless the director is personally aware of the relaxed atmosphere in which such a session can be conducted in (that phrase again) "real life." And while the director and performers will inevitably and rightly create their own interpretations, they must know what it is they are interpreting.

As for the style of the production itself, one can stage the play as it was staged in New York, which is to say, for a proscenium or thrust, with full and quite elaborate lights and set, seemingly simple in execution but not in their detail, or one can do the play environmentally. During rehearsal of WINGS for New York, it quickly became apparent to its director, John Madden, and to me, that the play could be very effectively staged with no light and sound changes at all! The key to all productions, it seems to me, is the eliciting of the audience's imaginative participation. And this can be done through lights and sound, in a traditional mode, or by very badly announcing that no quasi-realistic devises will be used at all. Mrs. Stilson's terrible isolation can be conveyed in many ways, and done skillfully and carefully, an audience will give its faith and attention to all of them.

Therefore, I urge the director to attend carefully to the play's stage directions and suggestions, but to trust his own theatrical instincts in production. The actors, theater, design limitations, all will suggest a mode of production. But while the play can be done many ways, I think it must always be done with great rigor and precision.

The basic step in designing a production is to find the appropriate theatrical analogs to Mrs. Stilson's condition; the script suggests one approach. There are others.

About the characters. Billy should not seem demented or in any way sinister. He is suffering from brain damage caused by an operation to remove a brain tumor; he is *almost* all right, and must appear likeable, jovial, and *almost normal.*

The patients in the speech therapy session are all happy to be there. Their rapport with Amy is profound and immediately apparent. Amy is intuitive.

About wheelchairs. In rehearsal, we found that putting Mrs. Stilson in a wheelchair (during her early convalescence) caused the audience to worry more about her ambulatory disabilities than her aphasia. For some reason, a wheelchair on stage is a mightier symbol than one in real life. We quickly abandoned it. (Perhaps, in an environmental production, the effect would be different. I pass this information on only so the director may be forewarned and prepared.)

September 1979

Arthur Kopit

CHARACTERS

EMILY STILSON

AMY, a therapist

DOCTORS

NURSES

BILLY, a patient

MR. BROWNSTEIN, a patient

MRS. TIMMINS, a patient

The play takes place over a period of two years; it should be performed without intermission.

NOTES ON THE PRODUCTION OF THIS PLAY

The stage as a void.

System of black scrim panels that can move silently and easily, creating the impression of featureless, labyrinthine corridors.

Some panels mirrored so they can fracture light, create the impression of endlessness, even airiness, multiply and confuse images, confound one's sense of space.

Sound both live and pre-recorded, amplified; speakers all around the theater.

No attempt should be made to create a literal representation of Mrs. Stilson's world, especially since Mrs. Stilson's world is no longer in any way literal.

The scenes should blend. No clear boundaries or domains in time or space for Mrs. Stilson any more.

It is posited by this play that the woman we see in the center of the void is the intact inner self of Mrs. Stilson. This inner self does not need to move physically when her external body (which we cannot see) moves. Thus, we infer movement from the context; from whatever clues we can obtain. It is the same for her, of course. She learns as best she can.

And yet, sometimes, the conditions change; then the woman we observe is Mrs. Stilson as others see her. We thus infer who it is we are seeing from the context, too. Sometimes we see both the inner and outer self at once.

Nothing about her world is predictable or consistent. This fact is its essence.

The progression of the play is from fragmentation to integration. By the end, boundaries have become somewhat clearer. But she remains always in another realm from us.

Prelude

*As audience enters, a cozy armchair visible Downstage in a
        pool of light, darkness surrounding it. A clock heard
        ticking in the dark. Lights to black. Hold.*

When the lights come back, EMILY STILSON, *a woman well
        into her seventies, is sitting in the armchair reading a
        book. Some distance away, a floor lamp glows dimly.
        On the other side of her chair, also some distance
        away, a small table with a clock. The chair, the lamp,
        and the table with the clock all sit isolated in narrow
        pools of light, darkness between and around them.
        The clock seems to be ticking a trifle louder than
        normal.*

MRS. STILSON, *enjoying her book and the pleasant evening,
        reads on serenely. And then she looks up. The lamp
        disappears into the darkness. But she turns back to her
        book as if nothing odd has happened; resumes read-
        ing. And then, a moment later, she looks up again, an
        expression of slight perplexity on her face. For no
        discernible reason, she turns toward the clock. The
        clock and the table it is sitting on disappear into the
        darkness. She turns front. Stares out into space. Then
        she turns back to her book. Resumes reading. But the
        reading seems an effort; her mind is on other things.
        The clock skips a beat. Only after the clock has re-
        sumed its normal rhythm does she look up. It is as if
        the skipped beat has only just then registered. For the
        first time, she displays what one might call concern.
        And then the clock stops again. This time the interval
        lasts longer. The book slips out of* MRS. STILSON'S
        hands; she stares out in terror. Blackout. Noise.

The moment of a stroke, even a relatively minor one, and its immediate aftermath, are an experience in chaos. Nothing at all makes sense. Nothing except perhaps this overwhelming disorientation will be remembered by the victim. The stroke usually happens suddenly. It is a catastrophe.

It is my intention that the audience recognize that some real event is occurring; that real information is being received by the victim, but that it is coming in too scrambled and too fast to be properly decoded. Systems overload.

And so this section must not seem like utter ''noise,'' though certainly it must be more noisy than intelligible. I do not believe there is any way to be true to this material if it is not finally ''composed'' in rehearsal, on stage, by ''feel.'' Theoretically, any sound or image herein described can occur anywhere in this section. The victim cannot process. Her familiar world has been rearranged. The puzzle is in pieces. All at once, and with no time to prepare, she has been picked up and dropped into another realm.

In order that this section may be put together in rehearsal (there being no one true ''final order'' to the images and sounds she perceives), I have divided this section into three discrete parts with the understanding that in performance these parts will blend together to form one cohesive whole.

The first group consists of the visual images Mrs. Stilson perceives.

The second group consists of those sounds emanating outside herself. Since these sounds are all filtered by her mind, and since her mind has been drastically altered, the question of whether we in the audience are hearing what is actually occurring or only hearing what she believes is occurring is unanswerable.

The third group contains Mrs. Stilson's words: the words she thinks and the words she speaks. Since we are perceiving the world through Mrs. Stilson's senses, there is no sure way for us to know whether she is actually saying any of these words aloud.

Since the experience we are exploring is not one of logic but its opposite, there is no logical reason for these groupings to occur in the order in which I have presented them. These are but components, building blocks, and can therefore be repeated, spliced, reversed, filtered, speeded up or slowed down. What should determine their final sequence and juxtaposition, tempi, intensity, is the "musical" sense of this section as a whole; it must pulse and build. An explosion quite literally is occurring in her brain, or rather, a series of explosions: the victim's mind, her sense of time and place, her sense of self, all are being shattered if not annihilated. Fortunately, finally, she will pass out. Were her head a pinball game it would register TILT—game over—stop. Silence. And resume again. Only now the victim is in yet another realm. The Catastrophe section is the journey or the fall into this strange and dreadful realm.

In the world into which Mrs. Stilson has been so violently and suddenly transposed, time and place are without definition. The distance from her old familiar world is immense. For all she knows, she could as well be on another planet.

In this new world, she moves from one space or thought or concept to another without willing or sometimes even knowing it. Indeed, when she moves in this maze-like place, it is as if the world around her and not she were doing all the moving. To her, there is nothing any more that is commonplace or predictable. Nothing is as it was. Everything comes as a surprise. Something has relieved her of command. Something beyond her comprehension has her in its grip.

In the staging of this play, the sense should therefore be conveyed of physical and emotional separation (by the use, for example, of the dark transparent screens through which her surrounding world can be only dimly and partly seen, or by alteration of external sound) and of total immersion in strangeness.

Because our focus is on Mrs. Stilson's inner self, it is important that she exhibit no particular overt physical disabilities. Furthermore, we should never see her in a wheelchair, even though, were we able to observe her through the doctors' eyes, a wheelchair is probably what she would, more often than not, be in.

One further note: because Mrs. Stilson now processes information at a different rate from us, there is no reason that what we see going on around her has to be the visual equivalent of what we hear.

Catastrophe

IMAGES	SOUNDS OUTSIDE HERSELF
	(SOUNDS *live or on tape, altered or unadorned.*)
	Of wind.
Mostly, it is whiteness. Dazzling, blinding.	
	Of someone breathing with effort, unevenly.
	Of something ripping, like a sheet.
Occasionally, there are brief rhombs of color, explosions of color, the color red being dominant.	*Of something flapping, the sound suggestive of an old screen door perhaps, or a sheet or sail in the wind. It is a rapid fibrillation. And it is used mostly to mark transitions. It can seem ominous or not.*
The mirrors, of course, reflect infinitely. Sense of endless space, endless corridors.	*Of a woman's scream (though this sound should be altered by filters so it resembles other things, such as sirens).*
	Of random noises recorded in a busy city hospital, then altered so as to be only minimally recognizable.
Nothing seen that is not a fragment. Every aspect of her world has been shattered.	*Of a car's engine at full speed.*

Mrs. Stilson's Voice

(VOICE *live or on tape,
altered or unadorned.*)

Oh my God oh my God oh
my God—

—trees clouds houses
mostly planes flashing past,
images without words, utter
disarray disbelief, never
seen this kind of thing
before!

Where am I? How'd I get
here?

My leg (What's my leg?)
feels wet arms . . . wet
too, belly same chin nose
everything (Where are they
taking me?) something
sticky (What has happened
to my plane?) feel
something sticky.

Doors! Too many doors!

32

IMAGES	SOUNDS OUTSIDE HERSELF
	Of a siren (altered to resemble a woman screaming).
Utter isolation.	*Of an airplane coming closer, thundering overhead, then zooming off into silence.*
In this vast whiteness, like apparitions, partial glimpses of doctors and nurses can be seen. They appear and disappear like a pulse. They are never in one place for long. The mirrors multiply their incomprehensibility.	*Of random crowd noises, the crowd greatly agitated. In the crowd, people can be heard calling for help, a doctor, an ambulance. But all the sounds are garbled.*
	Of people whispering.
	Of many people asking questions simultaneously, no question comprehensible.
	Of doors opening, closing, opening, closing.
Sometimes the dark panels are opaque, sometimes transparent. Always, they convey a sense of layers, multiplicity, separation. Sense constantly of doors opening, closing, opening, closing.	*Of someone breathing oxygen through a mask.*
	VOICES. (*Garbled.*) Just relax. / No one's going to hurt you. / Can you hear us?

MRS. STILSON'S VOICE

Must have . . . fallen
cannot . . . move at all
sky . . . (Gliding!) dark
cannot . . . talk (Feel as if
I'm gliding!).

Yes, feels cool, nice . . .
Yes, this is the life all right!

My plane! What has
happened to my plane!

Help . . .

—all around faces of which
nothing known no sense
ever all wiped out blank like
ice I think saw it once
flying over something some
place all was white sky and
sea clouds ice almost
crashed couldn't tell where
I was heading right side up
topsy-turvy under over I
was flying actually if I can I
do yes do recall was upside

34

IMAGES	SOUNDS OUTSIDE HERSELF
Fragments of hospital equipment appear out of nowhere and disappear just as suddenly. Glimpse always too brief to enable us to identify what this equipment is, or what its purpose.	/ Be careful! / You're hurting her! / No, we're not. / Don't lift her, leave her where she is! / Someone call an ambulance! / I don't think she can hear.
	MALE VOICE. Have you any idea—
	OTHER VOICES. (*Garbled.*) Do you know your name? / Do you know where you are? / What year is this? / If I say the tiger has been killed by the lion, which animal is dead?
Mrs. Stilson's movements seem random. She is a person wandering through space, lost.	
	A hospital paging system heard.
Finally, Mrs. Stilson is led by attendants downstage, to a chair. Then left alone.	*Equipment being moved through stone corridors, vast vaulting space. Endless echoing.*

down can you believe it almost scraped my head on
the ice caps couldn't tell
which way was up wasn't
even dizzy strange things
happen to me that they do!

What's my name? I don't
know my name!

Where's my arm? I don't
have an arm!

What's an arm?

AB-ABC-ABC123DE4512
12 what? 123—1234567897
2357 better yes no problem
I'm okay soon be out soon
be over storm . . . will
pass I'm sure. Always has.

Awakening

In performance, the end of the Catastrophe section should blend, without interruption, into the beginning of this.

MRS. STILSON *Downstage on a chair in a pool of light, darkness all around her. In the distance behind her, muffled sounds of a hospital. Vague images of* DOCTORS, NURSES *attending to someone we cannot see. One of the* DOCTORS *calls* MRS. STILSON's *name. Downstage,* MRS. STILSON *shows no trace of recognition. The* DOCTOR *calls her name again. Again no response. One of the* DOCTORS *says, "It's possible she may hear us but be unable to respond."*

One of the NURSES *tries calling out her name. Still no response. The* DOCTOR *leaves. The remaining* DOCTORS *and* NURSES *fade into the darkness. Only* MRS. STILSON *can be seen. Pause.*

MRS. STILSON. Still . . . sun moon too or . . . three times happened maybe globbidged rubbidged uff and firded-forded me to nothing there try again (*We hear a window being raised somewhere behind her.*) window! up and heard (*Sounds of birds.*) known them know I know them once upon a birds! that's it better getting better soon be out of this. (*Pause.*) Out of . . . what? (*Pause.*) Dark . . . space vast of . . . in I am or so it seems feels no real clues to speak of. (*Behind her, brief image of a* DOCTOR *passing.*) Something tells me I am not alone. Once! Lost it. No here back thanks work fast now, yes empty vast reach of space desert think they call it I'll come back to that anyhow down I . . . something what (*Brief image of a* NURSE.) it's SOMETHING ELSE IS ENTER-

39

ING MY!— no wait got it crashing OH MY GOD!
CRASHING! deadstick dead-of-night thought the stars
were airport lights upside down was I what a way to land
glad no one there to see it, anyhow tubbish blaxed and
vinkled I commenshed to uh-oh where's it gone to somewhere flubbished what? with (*Brief images of hospital staff
on the move.*) images are SOMETHING ODD IS! . . .
yes, then there I thank you crawling sands and knees still
can feel it hear the wind all alone somehow wasn't scared
why a mystery, vast dark track of space, we've all got to die
that I know, anyhow then day came light came with it so
with this you'd think you'd hope just hold on they will find
me I am . . . still intact. (*Pause.*) In here. (*Long silence.*)
Seem to be the word removed. (*Long silence.*) How long
have I been here? . . . And wrapped in dark. (*Pause.*)
Can remember nothing.

(*Outside sounds begin to impinge; same for images. In the
distance, an attendant dimly seen pushing a floor
polisher. Its noise resembles an animal's growl.*)

MRS. STILSON. (*Trying hard to be cheery.*) No, definitely
I am not alone! (*The sound of the polisher grows louder,
seems more bestial, voracious; it overwhelms everything.
Explosion! She gasps. Rapidly and in panic, sense of great
commotion behind her. A crisis has occurred.*) There I go
there I go hallway now it's screaming crowded pokes me
then the coolbreeze needle scent of sweetness can see palms
flowers flummers couldn't fix the leaking sprouting everywhere to save me help me CUTS UP THROUGH to something   movement   I   am   something   moving   without
movement!

(*Sound of a woman's muffled scream from behind her. The
scream grows louder.*)

MRS. STILSON. (*With delight.*) What a strange adventure I am having!

(*Lights to black on everything. In the dark, a pause. When her voice is heard again, it is heard first from all the speakers. Her voice sounds groggy, slurred. No longer any sense of panic discernible. A few moments after her voice is heard, the lights come up slowly on her. Soon, only she is speaking; the voice from the speakers has disappeared.*)

MRS. STILSON. Hapst aporkshop fleetish yes of course it's yes the good ol' times when we would mollis I mean collis all around still what my son's name is cannot for the life of me yet face gleams smiles as he tells them what I did but what his name is cannot see it pleasant anyway yes palms now ocean sea breeze wafting floating up and lifting holding weightless and goes swrooooping down with me least I . . . think it's me.

(*Sound of something flapping rapidly open and closed, open and closed. Sound of wind. Lights change into a cool and airy blue. Sense of weightlessness, serenity. In another realm now.*)

MRS. STILSON. Yes, out there walking not holding even danger ever-present how I loved it love it still no doubt will again hear them cheering wisht or waltz away to some place like Rumania . . . (*The wind disappears.*) Nothing . . . (*The serene blue light begins to fade away. Some place else now that she is going.*) Of course beyond that yet 1, 2 came before the yeast rose bubbled and MY CHUTE DIDN'T OPEN PROPERLY! Still for a girl did wonders getting down and it was Charles! no Charlie, who is Charlie? see him smiling as they tell him what I—

(Outside world begins to impinge. Lights are changing, growing brighter, something odd is happening. Sense of imminence. She notices.)

MRS. STILSON. *(Breathless with excitement.)* Stop hold cut stop wait stop come-out-break-out light can see it ready heart can yes can feel it pounding something underway here light is getting brighter lids I think the word is that's it lifting of their own but slowly knew I should be patient should be what? wait hold on steady now it's spreading no no question something underway here spreading brighter rising lifting light almost yes can almost there a little more now yes can almost see this . . . place I'm . . . in and . . . *(Look of horror.)* Oh my God! Now I understand! THEY'VE GOT ME!

(For first time doctors, nurses, hospital equipment all clearly visible behind her. All are gathered around someone we cannot see. From the way they are all bending over, we surmise this person we cannot see is lying in a bed. Lights drop on MRS. STILSON, Downstage.)

NURSE. *(Talking to the person Upstage we cannot see.)* Mrs. Stilson, can you open up your eyes? *(Pause.)*

MRS. STILSON. *(Separated from her questioners by great distance.)* Don't know how.

DOCTOR. Mrs. Stilson, you just opened up your eyes. We saw you. Can you open them again? *(No response.)* Mrs. Stilson . . . ?

MRS. STILSON. *(Proudly, triumphantly.)* My name then—Mrs. Stilson!

VOICE ON P.A. SYSTEM. Mrs. Howard, call on three! Mrs. Howard . . . !

MRS. STILSON. My name then—Mrs. Howard?

and I know it! What it is is a farmhouse made up to look like a hospital. Why? I'll come back to that. (*Enter another* NURSE.)

NURSE. Hi! Haven't seen you in a while. Have you missed me?

MRS. STILSON. (*No hint of recognition visible.*) What?

NURSE. (*Warmly.*) They say you didn't touch your dinner. Would you like some pudding?

MRS. STILSON. No.

NURSE. Good, I'll go get you some. (*Exit* NURSE, *very cheerfully.*)

MRS. STILSON. Yes no question they have got me I've been what that word was captured is it? No it's—Yes, it's captured how? Near as it can figure. I was in my prane and crashed, not unusual, still in all not too common. Neither is it very grub. Plexit rather or I'd say propopic. Well that's that, jungdaball! Anyhow to resume, what I had for lunch? That's not it, good books I have read, good what, done what? Whaaaaat? Do the busy here! Get inside this, rubbidge all around let the vontul do some yes off or it of above semilacrum pwooosh! what with noddygobbit nip-n-crashing inside outside witsit watchit funnel vortex sucking into backlash watchit get-out caught-in spinning ring-grab grobbit help woooosh! cannot stoppit on its own has me where it wants. (*And suddenly she is in another realm. Lights transformed into weightless blue. Sense of ease and serenity.*) Plane! See it thanks, okay, onto back we were and here it is. Slow down easy now. Captured. After crashing, that is what we said or was about to, think it so, cannot tell for sure, slow it slow it, okay here we go . . . (*Speaking slower now.*) captured after crashing by the enemy and brought here to this farm masquerading as a hospital. Why? For I would say offhand information. Of what sort though hard to tell. For example, questions such as can I raise my fingers, what's an overcoat, how many nickels in a rhyme, questions such as these. To what use can they be to the enemy? Hard to tell from here. Nonetheless, I would say must be certain information I possess that they want well I won't give it I'll escape! Strange things happen to me that they do! Good thing I'm all right! Must be in Rumania. Just a hunch of course. (*The serene blue light starts to fade.*) Ssssh, someone's coming.

(*A NURSE has entered. The NURSE guides MRS. STILSON to a DOCTOR. The blue light is gone. The NURSE leaves. The space MRS. STILSON now is in appears much more "real" and less fragmentary than what we have so far been observing. We see MRS. STILSON here as others see her.*)

DOCTOR. Mrs. Stilson, if you don't mind, I'd like to ask you some questions. Some will be easy, some will be hard. Is that all right?

MRS. STILSON. Oh yes I'd say oh well yes that's the twither of it.

DOCTOR. Good. Okay. Where were you born?

MRS. STILSON. Never. Not at all. Here the match wundles up you know and drats flames fires I keep careful always—

DOCTOR. Right . . . (*Speaking very slowly, precise enunciation.*) Where were you born?

MRS. STILSON. Well now well now that's a good thing knowing yushof course wouldn't call it such as I did andinjurations or aplovia could it? No I wouldn't think so. Next? (*Pause.*)

DOCTOR. Mrs. Stilson, are there seven days in a week?

MRS. STILSON. . . . Seven . . . Yes.

DOCTOR. Are there five days in a week? (*Pause.*)

MRS. STILSON. (*After much pondering.*) No.

DOCTOR. Can a stone float on water? (*Long pause.*)

MRS. STILSON. No.

DOCTOR. Mrs. Stilson, can you cough?

MRS. STILSON. Somewhat.

DOCTOR. Well, would you show me how you cough?

MRS. STILSON. Well now well now not so easy what you cromplie is to put these bushes open and—

DOCTOR. No no, Mrs. Stilson, I'm sorry—I would like to hear you cough.

MRS. STILSON. Well I'm not bort you know with plajits or we'd see it wencherday she brings its pillow with the fistils-opening I'd say outward always outward never stopping it. (*Long silence.*)

DOCTOR. Mrs. Stilson, I have some objects here. (*He takes a comb, a toothbrush, a pack of matches, and a key from his pocket, sets them down where she can see.*) Could you point to the object you would use for cleaning your teeth? (*Very long silence. Finally she picks up the comb and shows it to him. Then she puts it down. Waits.*) Mrs. Stilson, here, take this object in your hand. (*He hands her the toothbrush.*) Do you know what this object is called?

MRS. STILSON. (*With great difficulty.*) Tooooooooovvvv . . . bbbrum?

DOCTOR. Very good. Now put it down. (*She puts it down.*) Now, pretend you have it in your hand. Show me what you'd do with it. (*She does nothing.*) What does one do with an object such as that, Mrs. Stilson? (*No response.*) Mrs. Stilson, what is the name of the object you are looking at?

MRS. STILSON. Well it's . . . wombly and not at all . . . rigged or tuned like we might twunter or toring to work the clambness out of it or—

DOCTOR. Pick it up.

MRS. STILSON. (*As soon as she's picked it up.*) Tooovebram, tooove-britch bratch brush bridge, two-bridge.

DOCTOR. Show me what you do with it. (*For several moments she does nothing. then she puts it to her lips, holds it there motionless.*) Very good. Thank you.

(*She sighs heavily, puts it down. The* DOCTOR *gathers up his objects, leaves. Once again* MRS. STILSON *all alone. She stares into space. Then her voice is heard coming from all around; she herself does not speak.*)

HER VOICE. Dark now again out the window on my side lying here all alone . . . (*Very long silence.*)

MRS. STILSON. Yesterday my children came to see me. (*Pause.*) Or at least, I was told they were my children. Never saw them before in my life. (*She stares out, motionless. No expression. Then after a while she looks around. Studies the dark for clues.*) Time has become peculiar.

(*And she continues this scrutiny of the dark. But if this activity stems from curiosity, it is a mild curiosity at most. No longer does she convey or probably even experience the extreme, disoriented dread we saw earlier when she first arrived in this new realm. Her sense of urgency is gone. Indeed, were we able to observe* MRS. STILSON *constantly, we would inevitably conclude that her curiosity is now only minimally purposeful; that, in fact, more likely her investigations are the actions, possibly merely the reflex actions, of someone with little or nothing else to do. This is not to deny that she is desperately trying to piece her shattered world together. Undoubtedly, it is the dominant motif in her mind. But it is a motif probably more absent from her consciousness than present, and the quest it inspires is intermittent at best. Her mental abilities have not only been severely altered, they have been diminished: that is the terrible fact one cannot deny. And then suddenly she is agitated.*)

MRS. STILSON. Mother! . . . didn't say as she usually . . . (*Pause.*) And I thought late enough or early rather first light coming so when didn't move I poked her then with shoving but she didn't even eyes or giggle when I tickled. (*Pause.*) What it was was not a trick as I at first

had— (*Pause.*) Well I couldn't figure, he had never lied,
tried to get her hold me couldn't it was useless. Then his
face was, I had never known a face could . . . It was like
a mask then like sirens it was bursting open it was him then
I too joining it was useless. Can still feel what it was like
when she held me. (*Pause.*) So then well I was on my own.
He was all destroyed, had I think they say no strength for
this. (*Then she's silent. No expression. Stares into space.
Enter a* DOCTOR *and a* NURSE.)

DOCTOR. (*Warmly.*) Hello, Mrs. Stilson. (*He comes over
next to her. We cannot tell if she notices him or not. The*
NURSE, *chart in hand, stands a slight distance away.*)
You're looking much, much better. (*He smiles and sits
down next to her. He watches her for several moments,
searching for signs of recognition.*) Mrs. Stilson, do you
know why you're here?

MRS. STILSON. Well now well now . . . (*She gives it
up. Silence.*)

DOCTOR. You have had an accident—

MRS. STILSON.   DOCTOR.
(*Her words*   (*To all intents and
overpowering his.*)   *purposes, what he*
I don't trust him, don't trust   *says is lost.*)
anyone. Must get word out,   At home. Not in an
send a message where I am.   airplane. It's called a stroke.
Like a wall between me and   This means that your brain
others. No one ever gets it   has been injured and brain
right even though I tell them   tissue destroyed, though we
right. They are playing   are not certain of the cause.
tricks on me, two sides,   You could get better, and
both not my friends, goes in   you're certainly making
goes out too fast too fast   progress. But it's still too
hurts do the busy I'm all   soon to give any sort of
right I talk right why acting   exact prognosis. (*He studies
all these others like I don't, her. Then he rises and
what's he marking, what's   marks something on his
he writing?   clipboard.*)

(*Exit* DOCTOR *and* NURSE.)

MRS. STILSON. I am doing well of course! (*Pause. Secretive tone.*) They still pretend they do not understand me. I believe they may be mad. (*Pause.*) No they're not mad, I am mad. Today I heard it. Everything I speak is wronged. SOMETHING HAS BEEN DONE TO ME!

DOCTOR. (*Barely visible in the distance.*) Mrs. Stilson, can you repeat this phrase: "We live across the street from the school." (*She ponders.*)

MRS. STILSON. "Malacats on the forturay are the kesterfats of the romancers."

(*Look of horror comes across her face; the* DOCTOR *vanishes. Through the screens, Upstage, we see a* NURSE *bringing on a tray of food.*)

NURSE. (*Brightly.*) Okay ups-a-girl, ups-a-baby, dinnertime! Open wide now, mustn't go dribble-dribble—at's-a-way!

(MRS. STILSON *screams, swings her arms in fury. In the distance, Upstage, the tray of food goes flying.*)

MRS. STILSON. (*Screaming.*) Out! Get out! Take this shit away, I don't want it! Someone get me out of here!

NURSE. (*While* MRS. STILSON *continues shouting.*) Help, someone, come quick! She's talking! Good as you or me! It's a miracle! Help! Somebody! Come quick!

(*While* MRS. STILSON *continues to scream and flail her arms,* NURSES *and* DOCTORS *rush on Upstage and surround the patient we never see. And although* MRS. STILSON *continues to scream coherently, in fact she isn't any better, no miracle has occurred. Her ability to articulate with apparent normalcy has been brought*

*on by extreme agitation and in no way implies that she
could produce these sounds again "if she only
wanted"; will power has nothing to do with what we
hear. Her language, as it must, soon slips back into
jargon. She continues to flail her arms. In the back-
ground, we can see a* NURSE *preparing a
hypodermic.)*

MRS. STILSON. (*Struggling.*) —flubdgy please no-
mommy-callming holdmeplease to sleeEEEEP SHOOOOP
shop shnoper CRROOOOOCK SNANNING wuduitcoldly
should I gobbin flutter truly HELP ME yessisnofun, snofun,
wishes awhin dahd killminsilf if . . . could. (*In the distance, we see the needle given.*) OW! . . . would I
but . . . (*She's becoming drowsy.*) awful to me him as
well moas of all no cantduit . . . jusscantduit . . .

(*Head drops. Into sleep she goes. Exit* DOCTORS, NURSES.
*Sound of a gentle wind is heard. Lights fade to black
on* MRS. STILSON. *Darkness everywhere; the sound of
the wind fades away. Silence. Lights up on* AMY,
Downstage Right. Then lights up on MRS. STILSON
staring into space.)

AMY. Mrs. Stilson? (MRS. STILSON *turns toward the
sound, sees* AMY.) You have had what's called a stroke.

(*Change of lights and panels open. Sense of terrible en-
closure gone. Birds heard. We are outside now.* AMY
puts a shawl around MRS. STILSON's *shoulders.*)

AMY. Are you sure that will be enough?
MRS. STILSON. Oh yes . . . thhhankyou.

(*She tucks the shawl around herself. Then* AMY *guides her
through the panels as if through corridors; no rush,*

slow gentle stroll. They emerge other side of stage.
Warm light. AMY *takes in the view.* MRS. STILSON
appears indifferent.)

AMY. Nice to be outside, isn't it? . . . Nice view.

MRS. STILSON. (*Still with indifference.*) Yes indeed.
(*There are two chairs nearby, and they sit. Silence for a
time.*)

AMY. Are you feeling any better today? (*But she gets no
response. Then, a moment later,* MRS. STILSON *turns to*
AMY; *it is as if* AMY's *question has not even been heard.*)

MRS. STILSON. The thing is . . . (*But the statement
trails off into nothingness. She stares out, no expression.*)

AMY. Yes? What? (*Long silence.*)

MRS. STILSON. I can't make it do it like it used to.

AMY. Yes, I know. That's because of the accident.

MRS. STILSON. (*Seemingly oblivious of* AMY's *words.*)
The words, they go in somelimes then out they go, I can't
stop them here inside or make maybe globbidge to the tub-
berway or—

AMY. Emily. Emily!

MRS. STILSON. (*Shaken out of herself.*) . . . What?

AMY. Did you hear what you just said?

MRS. STILSON. . . . Why?

AMY. (*Speaking slowly.*) You must listen to what you're
saying.

MRS. STILSON. Did I . . . do . . .

AMY. (*Nodding, smiling; clearly no reproach intended.*)
Slow down. Listen to what you're saying. (*Silence.*)

MRS. STILSON. (*Slower.*) The thing is . . . doing all
this busy in here gets, you know with the talking it's like
. . . sometimes when I hear here (*She touches her head.*)
. . . but when I start to . . . kind more what kind of
voice should . . . it's like pfffft! (*She makes a gesture
with her hand of something flying away.*)

AMY. (*Smiling.*) Yes, I know. It's hard to find the words for what you're thinking of.

MRS. STILSON. Well yes. (*Long pause.*) And then these people, they keep waiting . . . And I see they're smiling and . . . they keep . . . waiting . . . (*Faint smile, helpless gesture. She stares off. Long silence.*)

AMY. Emily. (MRS. STILSON *looks up.*) Can you remember anything about your life . . . before the accident?

MRS. STILSON. Not sometimes, some days it goes better if I see a thing or smell . . . it . . . remembers me back, you see? And I see things that maybe they were me and maybe they were just some things you know that happens in the night when you . . . (*Struggling visibly.*) have your things closed, eyes.

AMY. A dream you mean.

MRS. STILSON. (*With relief.*) Yes. So I don't know for sure. (*Pause.*) If it was really me. (*Long silence.*)

AMY. Your son is bringing a picture of you when you were younger. We thought you might like that. (*No visible response. Long silence.*) You used to fly, didn't you?

MRS. STILSON. (*Brightly.*) Oh yes indeed! Very much! I walked . . . out . . . (*Pause. Softly, proudly.*) I walked out on wings. (*Lights fade on* AMY. MRS. STILSON *alone again.*) Sitting here on my bed I can close my eyes shut out all that I can't do with, hearing my own talking, others, names that used to well just be there when I wanted now all somewhere else. No control. Close my eyes then, go to— (*Sound of something flapping rapidly. A fibrillation. Lights become blue. Sense of weightlessness, serenity.*) Here I go. No one talks here. Images coming I seem feel it feels better this way here is how it goes: this time I am still in the middle Stilson in the middle going out walking out wind feels good hold the wires feel the hum down below far there they are now we turn it bank it now we spin! Looks more bad than really is, still needs good balance and those nerves and that thing that courage thing don't fall off! . . . And now I'm out . . . and back and . . . (*With surprise.*) there's the window. (*Lights have returned to normal. She is back where she started.* AMY *enters.*)

AMY. Hello, Emily.

MRS. STILSON. Oh, Amy! . . . Didn't hear what you was . . . coming here to . . . Oh!

AMY. What is it?

MRS. STILSON. Something . . . wet.

AMY. Do you know what it is?

MRS. STILSON. Don't . . . can't say find it word.

AMY. Try. You can find it.

MRS. STILSON. Wet . . . thing, many, both sides yes.

AMY. Can you name them? What they are? You do know what they are. (*Pause.*)

MRS. STILSON. . . . Tears?

AMY. That's right, very good. Those are tears. And do you know what that means?

MRS. STILSON. . . . Sad?

AMY. Yes, right, well done, it means . . . that you are sad.

Explorations

Stage dark. In the dark, a piano heard: someone fooling
around on the keyboard, brief halting snatches of old
songs emerging as the product; would constitute a
medley were the segments only longer, more cohesive.
As it is, suspicion aroused that what we hear is all the
pianist can remember. Sound of general laughter, hub-
bub. Lights rise.

What we see is a rec room, in some places clearly, in others
not (the room being observed partly through the dark
scrim panels). Upstage Right, an upright piano, play-
ers and friends gathered round. Doctors, therapists,
nurses, attendants, patients, visitors certainly are not
all seen, but those we do see come from such a group.
We are in the rec room of a rehabilitation center. Some
patients in wheelchairs. The room itself has bright
comfortable chairs, perhaps a card table, magazine
rack, certainly a TV set. Someone now turns on the
TV.

What emerges is the sound of Ella Fitzgerald in live per-
formance. She sings scat: mellow, upbeat. The
patients and staff persuade the pianist to cease. Ella's
riffs of scat cast something like a spell.

MRS. STILSON *wanders through the space. The rec room, it*
should be stressed, shows more detail and color than
any space we've so far seen. Perhaps a vase of flowers
helps to signal that MRS. STILSON's *world is becoming*
fuller, more integrated. Movements too seem normal,
same for conversations that go on during all of this,
though too softly for us to comprehend. The music of
course sets the tone. All who listen are in its thrall.

New time sense here, a languor almost. The dread MRS.

STILSON *felt has been replaced by an acknowledgment of her condition, though not an understanding. In this time before she speaks, and in fact during, we observe the life of the rec room behind and around her. This is not a hospital any more, and a kind of normalcy prevails. The sense should be conveyed of corridors leading to and from this room.*

Then the music and the rec room sounds grow dim; MRS. STILSON *comes forward, lost in the drifts of a thought.*

MRS. STILSON. (*Relaxed, mellow.*) Wonder . . . what's inside of it . . . ? (*Pause.*) I mean, how does it work? What's inside that . . . makes it work? (*Long pause. She ponders.*) I mean when you . . . think about it all . . . (*Pause.*) And when you think that it could . . . ever have been . . . possible to . . . be another way . . .

(*She ponders. But it's hard for her to keep in mind what she's been thinking of, and she has to fight the noise of the rec room, its intrusive presence. Like a novice juggler,* MRS. STILSON *is unable to keep outside images and inner thoughts going simultaneously. When she's with her thoughts, the outside world fades away. When the outside world is with her, her thoughts fade away. But she fights her way through it, and keeps the thought in mind. The rec room, whose noise has just increased, grows quiet.*)

MRS. STILSON. Maybe . . . if somehow I could— (*She searches for the words that match her concept.*) — get inside . . . (*Pause. Sounds of the rec room pulse louder. She fights against it. The rec room sounds diminish.*) Prob'ly . . . very dark inside . . . (*She ponders; tries to picture what she's thinking.*) Yes . . . twisting kind of place I bet . . . (*Ponders more.*) With lots of . . . (*She searches for the proper word; finds it.*) passageways that

. . . lead to . . . (*Again, she searches for the word. The outside world rushes in.*)

PATIENT IN A WHEELCHAIR. (*Only barely audible.*) My foot feels sour. (*An attendant puts a lap rug over the patient's limbs. Then the rec room, once again, fades away.*)

MRS. STILSON. (*Fighting on.*) . . . lead to . . . something . . . Door! Yes . . . closed off now I . . . guess possib . . . ly for good I mean . . . forever, what does that mean? (*She ponders.*)

ATTENDANT. Would you like some candy?

MRS. STILSON. No.

ATTENDANT. Billy made it.

MRS. STILSON. No! (*The* ATTENDANT *moves back into the shadows.*) Where was I? (*She looks around.*) Why can't they just . . . let me . . . be when I'm . . . (*Lights start to change. Her world suddenly in flux. The rec room fades from view. Sounds of birds heard, dimly at first. Aware of the change as it is occurring.*) okay. Slipping out of . . . it and . . . (MRS. STILSON *in a different place.*) Outside now! How . . . did I do that?

AMY. (*Emerging from the shadows.*) Do you like this new place better?

MRS. STILSON. Oh well oh well yes, much, all . . . nice flowers here, people seem . . . more like me. Thank you. (AMY *moves back toward the shadows.*) And then I see it happen once again . . . (AMY *gone from sight.*) Amy kisses me. Puts her—what thing is it, arm! yes, arm, puts her arm around my . . . (*Pause.*) shoulder, turns her head away so I can't . . . (*Pause.*) Well, it knows what she's doing. May not get much better even though I'm here. No, I know that. I know that. No real need for her to . . . (*Long pause.*) Then she kisses me again. (*Pause.*) Walks away . . .

(*Pause. Lights change again, world again in flux. Noises of the building's interior can be heard like a babel, only fleetingly coherent. The rec room seen dissolving.*)

MRS. STILSON. Where am I? (*She begins to wander through a maze of passageways. The mirrors multiply her image, create a sense of endlessness.*)

(*NOTE. The following blocks of sound, which accompany her expedition, are meant to blend and overlap in performance and, to that end, can be used in any order and combined in any way desired, except for the last five blocks, numbers 12-16, which must be performed in their given sequence and in a way that is comprehensible. The sounds themselves may be live or pre-recorded; those which are pre-recorded should emanate from all parts of the theater and in no predictable pattern. The effect should be exhilarating and disorienting. An adventure. With terrifying aspects to be sure. But the sense of mystery and adventure must never be so overwhelmed by the terror that it is either lost altogether or submerged to the point of insignificance.* MRS. STILSON *may be frightened here, but the fear does not prevent her from exploring. She wanders through the labyrinth of dark panels as if they were so many doors, each door leading into yet another realm.*)

BLOCK 1. It was but a few years later that Fritsch and Hitzig stimulated the cortex of a dog with an electric current. Here at last was dramatic and indisputable evidence that—

BLOCK 2. Would you like me to change the channel?

BLOCK 3. . . . . presented, I would say, essentially similar conclusions on the behavioral correlates of each cerebral convolution.

BLOCK 4. (*Being the deep male voice, speaking slowly, enunciating carefully, that one hears on the speech-therapy machine known as "The Language Master."*) Mother led Bud to the bed.

BLOCK 5. . . . In the laboratory then, through electrical stimulation of neural centers or excisions of areas of the brain, scientists acquired information about the organization of mental activities in the monkey, the dog, the cat, and the rat. The discovery of certain peculiar clinical pictures, reminiscent of bizarre human syndromes, proved of special interest.

BLOCK 6. Can you tell me what this object's called?

BLOCK 7. Ella's riffs of scat, as if we were still in the rec room after all.

BLOCK 8. One has only to glance through the writings of this period to sense the heightened excitement attendant upon these discoveries!

BLOCK 9. Possibly some diaschisis, which would of course help account for the apparent mirroring. And then, of course, we must not overlook the fact that she's left-handed.

BLOCK 10. Of course, you understand, these theories may all be wrong! (*Sound of laughter from an audience.*) Any other questions? Yes, over there, in the corner.

BLOCK 11. Mrs. Stilson, this is Dr. Rogans. Dr. Rogans, this is Emily Stilson.

BLOCK 12. (*Male voice.*) —definite possibility I would say of a tiny subclinical infarct in Penfield's area. Yes? (*Female Voice.*) Are you sure there is a Penfield's area? (*Male Voice.*) No. (*Laughter from his audience. Male Voice again, itself on the verge of laughter.*) But *something* is wrong with her! (*Raucous laughter from his audience.*)

(*NOTE. Emerging out of the laughter in* BLOCK *12, a single musical TONE. This tone increases in intensity. It should carry through* BLOCK *16 and into* MRS. STILSON'S *emergence from the maze of panels, helping to propel her into the realm and the memory to which this expedition has been leading.*)

BLOCK 13. The controversy, of course, is that some feel it's language without thought, and others, thought without language . . .

BLOCK 14. What it is, of course, is the symbol system. Their symbol system's shot. They can't make analogies.

BLOCK 15. You see, it's all so unpredictable. There are no fixed posts, no clear boundaries. The victim, you could say, has been cut adrift . . .

BLOCK 16. Ah, now you're really flying blind there!

(MRS. STILSON *emerges from the maze of corridors. Sound perhaps of wind, or bells. Lights blue, sense again of weightlessness, airiness.*)

MRS. STILSON. (*In awe and ecstasy.*) As I see it now, the plane was flying BACKWARDS! Really, wind that strong, didn't know it could be! Yet the sky was clear, not a cloud, crystal blue, gorgeous, angels could've lived in sky like that . . . I think the cyclone must've blown in on the Andes from the sea . . . (*Blue light fades. Wind gone, bells gone, musical tone is gone. Coming out of it.*) Yes . . . (*She looks around; gets her bearings.*) Yes, no question, this . . . place better. (*And now she's landed.*) All these people just . . . like me, I guess.

(*She takes in where she is, seems slightly stunned to be back where she started. Sense of wonderment apparent. An attendant approaches.*)

ATTENDANT. Mrs. Stilson?
MRS. STILSON. (*Startled.*) Oh!
ATTENDANT. Sorry to—
MRS. STILSON. Is it . . . ?
ATTENDANT. Yes.
MRS. STILSON. Did I . . . ?
ATTENDANT. No, no need to worry. Here, I'll take you.

(*The* ATTENDANT *guides* MRS. STILSON *to a therapy room,
though, in fact, more likely [on the stage] the room
assembles around her. In the room are* AMY, BILLY [*a
man in his middle thirties*], MRS. TIMMINS [*elderly, in
a wheelchair*], *and* MR. BROWNSTEIN [*also elderly
and in a wheelchair*]. *The* ATTENDANT *leaves*.)

AMY. Well! Now that we're all here on this lovely afternoon, I thought that maybe—
BILLY. She looks really good.
AMY. What?
BILLY. This new lady here, can't remember what her
name is, no bother, anyhow, she looks really nice all
dressed like this, an' I jus' wanna extent a nice welcome
here on behalf o' all of us. (*The other patients mumble their
assent.*)
AMY. Well, that is very nice, Billy, very nice. Can any of
the rest of you remember this woman's name?
BILLY. I seen her I think when it is, yesterday, how's
that?
AMY. Very good, that's right, you met her for the first
time yesterday. Now, can any of you remember her name?
BILLY. Dolores.
AMY. (*Laughing slightly.*) No, not Dolores.
MR. BROWNSTEIN. She vas, I caught sight ya know,
jussaminute, flahtied or vhat, vhere, midda (*He hums a
note.*) —
AMY. Music.
MR. BROWNSTEIN. Yeah right goodgirlie right she vas
lissning, I caught slight, saw her vooding bockstond
tipping-n-topping de foot vas jussnow like dis. (*He starts to
stamp his foot.*)
AMY. Mrs. Stilson, were you inside listening to some
music just now?
MRS. STILSON. Well . . . (*Pause. Very fast.*) Well now
I was yes in the what in-the-in-the where the—

AMY. (*Cheerfully.*) Sssssllllow dowwwwwn. (*The other patients laugh;* MRS. TIMMINS *softly echoes the phrase "slow down." Speaking very slowly.*) Listen to yourself talking.

MRS. STILSON. (*Speaking slowly.*) Well yes, I was . . . listening and it was it was going in . . . good I think, I'd say, very good yes I liked it very nice it made it very nice inside.

AMY. Well, good.

MRS. TIMMINS. Applawdgia!

AMY. Ah, Mrs. Timmins! You heard the music, too?

MRS. TIMMINS. (*With a laugh.*) Ohshorrrrrrn. Yossssso, TV.

AMY. Well, good for you! Anyway, I'd like you all to know that this new person in our group is named Mrs. Stilson.

MR. BROWNSTEIN. Sssssstaa-illlllsssim.

AMY. Right! Well done, Mr. Brownstein!

MR. BROWNSTEIN. (*Laughing proudly.*) It's vurk-tiddiDINGobitch!

AMY. That's right it's working, I told you it would.

BILLY. Hey! Wait, hold on here—jus' remembered!

AMY. What's that, Billy?

BILLY. You've been holdin' out pay up where is it?

AMY. Where . . . is what?

BILLY. Where is for all what I did all that time labor which you—don't kid me, I see you grinning back there ate up (*He makes munching sounds.*) so where is it, where's the loot?

AMY. For the cheesecake.

BILLY. That's right you know it for the cheesecape, own recipe, extra-special, pay up.

AMY. (*To* MRS. STILSON.) Billy is a terrific cook.

MRS. STILSON. (*Delighted.*) Oh!

BILLY. Well used t' be, not now much what they say, anyhow, hah-hah! see? look, laughing, giggles, tries t' hide it, she knows she knows, scoundrel, thief, can't sleep nights

can you, people give their arms whatnots recipe like that
one is. Cheapskate. Come on fork over hand it over, don't
be chief.

AMY. . . . What?

BILLY. Don't be chief. (*Pause.*) You know, when someone don' pay, you say he's chief.

AMY. (*Warmly, nearly laughing.*) Billy, you're not
listening.

BILLY. Okay not the word not the right word what's the
word? I'll take any help you can give me. (*He laughs.*)

AMY. Cheap.

BILLY. That's it that's the word that's what you are, from
now on I'm gonna sell my recipes somewheres else.

AMY. Billy, say cheap. (*He sighs mightily.*)

BILLY. . . . Chief. (*Her expression tells him everything.*) Not right okay, try again this thing we can, what's
its, lessee okay here we go CHARF! Nope. Not right. Ya
know really, this could take all day.

AMY. Well then, the sooner you do it, the sooner we can
go on to what I've planned.

BILLY. You've got somethin' planned? You've never got
somethin' planned.

AMY. I've *always* got something planned.

BILLY. Oh come on don' gimme that, you're jus' tryin' to
impress this new lady, really nice new lady, Mrs. . . .

AMY. Stilson.

BILLY. Yeah her, you're jus' tryin'—what's that word
again?

AMY. Cheap.

BILLY. Cheap right okay lessee now—

AMY. Billy! You just said it!

BILLY. Did I? Good. Then maybe we can go on to somethin' else, such as when you're gonna fork over for the
cheesecake, I could be a rich man now.

AMY. Billy, I never made the cheesecake.

BILLY. I'll bet you've gone sold the recipe to all the

stores the whatnot everywhere fancy bigdeal places made a fortune, gonna retire any day t' your farm in New Jersey.

AMY. I don't have a farm in New Jersey, *you* have a farm in New Jersey!

BILLY. Oh? Then what were you doin' on my farm then?

AMY. I wasn't on your farm, Billy, I've been here! (BILLY *starts arguing about something incomprehensible and seemingly unrelated to farm life, the argument consisting mostly of the recitation of a convoluted string of numbers;* AMY *cuts him short before he goes too far astray.*) Billy, cheap, say cheap! (*Long silence.*)

BILLY. (*Simply and without effort.*) Cheap. (AMY *cheers. Overjoyed.*) Cheap!— Cheap-cheap-cheap-cheap-cheap!

MR. BROWNSTEIN. I vas hoping you could polsya and git vid mustard all dis out of dis you gottit right good I say hutchit and congratulupsy!

AMY. Congratu*lations*.

MR. BROWNSTEIN. Yeah right dassit goodgirlie, phhhhew! fin'lly!

(*Lights fade to black all around* MRS. STILSON. *Nothing seen but her. Silence for a time.*)

MRS. STILSON. What it was . . . how I heard it how I said it not the same, you would think so but it's not. Sometimes . . . well it just goes in so fast, in-and-out all the sounds. I know they mean— (*Pause.*) I mean I know they're . . . well like with me, helping, as their at their in their best way knowing how I guess they practice all the time so I'd say must be good or even better, helps me get the dark out just by going you know sssslowww and thinking smiling . . . it's not easy. (*Pause.*) Sometimes . . . how can . . . well it's just I think these death things, end it, stuff like sort of may be better not to listen anything no more at all or trying even talking cause what good's it, I'm so far away! Well it's crazy I don't mean it I don't think, still it's just like clouds that you can push through. Still you do it, still you try to. I can't hear things same as others say them. (*Pause.*) So the death thing, it comes in, I don't ask it, it just comes in, plays around in there, I can't get it out till it's ready, goes out on its own. Same I guess for coming. I don't open up the door.

(*Silence. Lights up on a chair, small table. On the table, a cassette recorder.* MRS. STILSON *goes to the chair. Sits. Stares at the recorder. A few moments later,* BILLY *and a* DOCTOR *enter.*)

BILLY. Oh, I'm sorry, I didn't know you was in . . . here or . . .

MRS. STILSON. Dr. Freedman said I could . . . use room and his . . . this . . . (*She gestures toward the recorder.*)

DOCTOR. No problem, we'll use another room.

(*He smiles. Exit* BILLY *and* DOCTOR. MRS. STILSON *turns back to the machine. Stares at it. Then she reaches out, presses a button.*)

DOCTOR'S VOICE. (*From cassette recorder.*) All right, essentially, a stroke occurs when there's a stoppage . . . When blood flow ceases in one part of the brain . . . And that brain can no longer get oxygen . . . And subsequently dies. Okay? Now, depending upon which part of the brain is affected by the stroke, you'll see differences in symptoms. Now what you've had is a left cerebral infarction. Oh, by the way, you're doing much, much better. We were very worried when you first arrived . . .

(*Silence. She clicks off the recording machine. Does nothing, stares at nothing. Then she reaches out and pushes the rewind button. The machine rewinds to start of tape. Stops automatically. She stares at the machine. Deep breath. Reaches out again. Presses the playback button.*)

DOCTOR'S VOICE. All right, essentially, a stroke occurs when there's a stoppage . . . When blood flow ceases in one part of the brain . . . And that brain can no long— (*She shuts it off. Stares into space. Silence.*)

(MRS. STILSON *with* AMY *sitting next to her on another chair.*)

MRS. STILSON. (*Still staring into space.*) "Memory" . . . (*Pause.*)

AMY. Yes, come on, "memory" . . . (*No response.*) Anything. (*Still no response. Warmly.*) Oh, come on, I bet there are lots of things you can talk about . . . You've been going out a lot lately . . . With your son . . . With your niece . . . (*Pause.*) What about Rhinebeck? Tell me about Rhinebeck. (*Pause.*)

MRS. STILSON. On . . . Saturday . . . (*She ponders.*) On . . . Sunday my . . . son . . . (*Ponders again.*) On Saturday my son . . . took me to see them out at Rhinebeck.

AMY. See what?

MRS. STILSON. What I used to . . . fly in.

AMY. Can you think of the word?

MRS. STILSON. . . . What word?

AMY. For what you used to fly in. (*Long pause.*)

MRS. STILSON. Planes!

AMY. Very good!

MRS. STILSON. Old . . . planes.

AMY. That is very good. Really!

MRS. STILSON. I sat . . . inside one of them. He said it was like the kind I used to . . . fly in and walk . . . out on wings in. I couldn't believe I could have ever done this.

(*Pause.*) But he said I did, I had. He was very . . . proud.
(*Pause.*) Then . . . I saw my hand was pushing on this
. . . stick . . . Then my hand was . . . pulling. Well I
hadn't you know asked my hand to do this, it just went and
did it on its own. So I said okay Emily, if this is how it
wants to do it you just sit back here and watch . . . But
. . . my head, it was really . . . hurting bad. And I was
up here both . . . sides, you know . . .

AMY. Crying.

MRS. STILSON. (*With effort.*) Yeah. (*Long pause.*) And
then all at once—it remembered everything! (*Long pause.*)
But now it doesn't. (*Silence.*)

(*Faint sound of wind. Hint of bells. The screens open. We
are outside. Sense of distance, openness. All feeling of
constraint is gone. AMY helps MRS. STILSON into an
overcoat; AMY is in an overcoat already.*)

AMY. Are you sure you'll be warm enough?
MRS. STILSON. Oh yes . . .

(*And they start to walk—a leisurely stroll through a park or
meadow, sense of whiteness everywhere. They head
toward a bench with snow on its slats. The sound of
wind grows stronger. Faint sound of an airplane over-
head, the sound quickly disappearing.*)

MRS. STILSON. This is winter, isn't it?
AMY. Yes.
MRS. STILSON. That was just a guess, you know.
AMY. (*With a warm, easy laugh.*) Well, it was a good
one, keep it up! (MRS. STILSON *laughs.* AMY *stops by the
bench.*) Do you know what this is called?
MRS. STILSON. Bench!
AMY. Very good! No, I mean what's on top of it. (*No
response.*) What I'm brushing off . . . (*Still no response.*)
What's falling from the sky . . . (*Long silence.*)

MRS. STILSON. Where do you get names from?

AMY. I? From in here, same as you.

MRS. STILSON. Do you know how you do it?

AMY. No.

MRS. STILSON. Then how am I supposed . . . to learn?

AMY. (*Softly*.) I don't really know.

(MRS. STILSON *stares at* AMY. *Then she points at her and laughs. At first,* AMY *doesn't understand. Then she does. And then both of them are laughing.*)

MRS. STILSON. Look. You see? (*She scoops some snow off the bench.*) If I pick this . . . stuff up in my hand, then . . . I know its name. I didn't have to pick it up to know . . . what it *was*.

AMY. No . . .

MRS. STILSON. But to find its name . . . (*She stares at what is in her hand.*) I had to pick it up.

AMY. What's its name?

MRS. STILSON. Snow. It's really nuts, isn't it!

AMY. It's peculiar! (*They laugh. Then, laughter gone, they sit; stare out. Silence for a time.*)

MRS. STILSON. A strange thing happened to me . . . (*Pause.*) I think last night.

AMY. Can you remember it?

MRS. STILSON. Perfectly.

AMY. Ah!

MRS. STILSON. I think it may have been . . . you know, when you sleep . . .

AMY. A dream.

MRS. STILSON. Yes, one of those, but I'm not . . . sure that it was . . . that. (*Pause. Then she notices the snow in her hand.*) Is it all right if I . . . eat this?

AMY. Yes! We used to make a ball of it, then pour maple syrup on top. Did you ever do that?

MRS. STILSON. I don't know. (*Pause.*) No, I remember—

I did! (*She tastes the snow. Smiles. After a time, the smile vanishes. She turns back to* AMY.) Who was that man yesterday?

AMY. What man?

MRS. STILSON. In our group. He seemed all right.

AMY. Oh, that was last week.

MRS. STILSON. I thought for sure he was all right! I thought he was maybe, you know, a doctor.

AMY. Yes, I know.

MRS. STILSON. (*Searching her memory.*) And you asked him to show you where his . . . hand was.

AMY. And he knew.

MRS. STILSON. That's right, he raised his hand, he knew. So I thought, why is Amy joking? (*She ponders.*) Then you asked him . . . (*She tries to remember.*) where . . . (*She turns to* AMY.)

AMY. His elbow was.

MRS. STILSON. Yes! And he . . . (*She struggles to find the word.*)

AMY. (*Helping.*) Pointed—

MRS. STILSON. (*At the same time.*) Pointed! to . . . (*But the struggle's getting harder.*)

AMY. The corner of the room.

MRS. STILSON. Yes. (*Pause. Softly.*) That was very . . . scary.

AMY. Yes. (MRS. STILSON *stares into space. Silence.*) What is it that happened to you last night?

MRS. STILSON. Oh yes! Well, this . . . *person* . . . came into my room. I couldn't tell if it was a man or woman or . . . young or old. I was in my bed and it came. Didn't seem to have to walk just . . . came over to my . . . bed and . . . smiled at where I was. (*Pause.*) And then it said . . . (*In a whisper.*) "Emily . . . we're glad you changed your mind." (*Pause.*) And then . . . it turned and left.

AMY. Was it a doctor? (MRS. STILSON *shakes her head.*)

One of the staff? (Mrs. Stilson *shakes her head.*) How do you know?

Mrs. Stilson. I just know. (*Pause.*) Then . . . I left my body.

Amy. *What?*

Mrs. Stilson. (*With great excitement.*) I was on the . . . what's the name over me—

Amy. Ceiling?

Mrs. Stilson. Yes! I was floating like a . . .

Amy. Cloud? (Mrs. Stilson *shakes her head.*) Bird?

Mrs. Stilson. Yes, up there at the— (*She searches for the word; finds it.*) ceiling, and I looked down and I was still there in my bed! Wasn't even scared, which you'd think I would be . . . And I thought, wow! this is the life isn't it? (*Sound of wind. Lights begin to change.* Amy *recedes into the darkness.*) It comes now without my asking . . . Amy is still beside me but I am somewhere else. I'm not scared. It has taken me, and it's clear again. Something is about to happen. (*Pause.* Amy *now completely gone.* Mrs. Stilson *in a narrow spot of light, darkness all around.*) I am in a plane, a Curtiss Jenny, and it's night. Winter. Snow is falling. Feel the tremble of the wings! How I used to walk out on them! Could I have really done—Yes. What I'd do, I'd strap myself with a tether to the stays, couldn't see the tether from below, then out I'd climb! Oh my, but it was wonderful! I could feel the wind! shut my eyes, all alone— FEEL THE SOARING!

(*The wind grows stronger. Then the wind dies away. Silence. She notices the change.*)

Mrs. Stilson. But this is in another time. Where I've been also . . . It is night and no one else is in the plane. Is it . . . remembering? (*Pause.*) No . . . No, I'm simply there again! (*Pause.*) And I'm lost . . . I am lost, completely lost, have to get to . . . somewhere, Omaha I think. The radio is out, or rather for some reason picks up only Bucharest. Clouds all around, no stars only snow, don't possess a clue to where I am, flying blind, soon be out of gas . . . And then the clouds open up a bit, just a bit, and lights appear below, faint, a hint, like torches. Down I drop! heart pounding with relief, with joy, hoping for a landing place, I'll take anything—a field, a street, and down I drop! No place to land . . . It's a town but the smallest—one tiny street is all, three street lamps, no one on the street, all deserted . . . just a street and some faint light in the middle of darkness. Nothing. Still, down I go! Maybe I can find a name on a railroad station, find out where I am! . . . But I see nothing I can read . . . So I begin to circle, though I know I'm wasting fuel and I'll crash if I keep this up! But somehow, I just can't tear myself away! Though I know I should pull back on the stick, get the nose up, head north into darkness—Omaha must be north! But no, I keep circling this one small silly street in this one small town . . . I'm scared to leave it, that's what, as if I guess once away from it I'll be inside something empty, black, and endless . . . (*Pause.*) So I keep circling—madness!—but I love it, what I see below! And I just can't bring myself to give it up, it's that simple—just can't bring myself to give it up! (*Pause.*) Then I know I have to. It's a luxury I can't afford. Fuel is running low, almost gone, may be too late anyway, so— (*Pause.*) I pull the nose up, kick the rudder, bank, and head out into darkness all in terror! GOD, BUT IT TAKES EFFORT! JUST DON'T WANT TO DO IT! . . . But I do. (*Pause. Suddenly calm.*) Actually, odd thing, once I did, broke free, got into the dark, found I wasn't even scared . . . Or was I? (*Slight laugh.*) Can't remember . . . Wonder where that town was . . . ? (*Pause.*) Got to Omaha all right. (*Pause.*) Was it Omaha . . . ? (*Pause.*) Yes, I think so . . . Yes, Topeka, that was it! (*Pause.*) God, but it was wonderful! (*Slight laugh.*) Awful scary sometimes, though!

(AMY *seen in the distance*.)

AMY. Emily! Emily, are you all right? (*Sudden, sharp, terrifying flapping sound.* MRS. STILSON *gasps.* AMY *disappears*.)

MRS. STILSON. (*Rapidly.*) Around! There here spins saw it rumple chumps and jumps outgoes inside up and . . . takes it, gives it, okay . . . (*Pause. Easier.*) Touch her for me, would you? (*Pause. Even easier.*) Oh my, yes, and here it goes then out . . . there I think on . . . wings? Yes . . . (*Pause. Softly, faint smile.*) Thank you. (*No trace of terror. Music. Hint of bells. Lights to black. Silence.*)

PROPERTY LIST

Prop Preset

On Stage
Stuffed armchair with pillow C.
End table with doily, clock, glass U.R.
Floor lamp U.L.
(All panels flush front—Carpenter)
(R. and L. triptic mirror open, C. triptic mirror closed—Carpenter)
(Glow tape charged up—Stage Manager)

Off Stage Right
2 grey metal chairs
Bed-table with pillow
Park bench with snow
2 wood-frame chairs (blue, gold)
Wheel chair (green)
Intravenous unit
Tray with cup, saucer, bowl, dish, cover, knife, fork, spoon
Floral bouquet
Candy tin with candy
Big clipboard with score sheet

Off Stage Left
2 grey metal chairs
Grey metal armchair
Typewriter table with cassette player (rewound)
Portable TV
Wood-frame chair (gold)
Wheel chair (blue)
Trolly with syringe, hospital supplies

77

Book
Small clipboard with score sheet
(2 coats and scarf—Wardrobe Supervisor)

Personal FIRST DOCTOR
Pen, pencil, toothbrush, comb, key, quarter

Personal SECOND DOCTOR
Pen

PROP MOVES

Liam

Preset out: Enter L.1, walk
   Constance to C., open
   panel 3 for her, close,
   exit R.1 corner.

House Man

Lamp out: Enter L.2,
   strike lamp L.2.

Black out: Enter D.R., strike
   armchair and book D.L.

Black out: Enter L.1, strike
   end table R.1.

Chaos: Enter L.3, follow
   nurses D.C., set grey
   chair spike #1, cross U.,
   close panels 23, exit L.
   3 corner.

"This is grotesque!" Enter
   L.1, move grey chair U.
   to spike #2, exit L.1.

Cue light: Enter D.R., set
   grey chair spike #3,
   cross U., cross C. through
   1, strike grey chair L.1.

Cue light: Enter D.R., set
   bed-table spike #3, exit
   D.R.

Cue light: Enter D.L., set 2
   grey chairs spike #4,
   cross U., cross R. through
   1, cross D., strike grey
   chair D.R.

Cue light: Enter D.R., strike
   bed-table D.R.

79

Cue light: Enter D.L., strike empty grey chair D.L.

Cue light: Enter D.R., set grey chair spike #5, exit D.R., set grey chair spike #5, exit D.R.

Cue light: Enter D.L., strike grey chair D.L.

Cue light: Enter D.R., strike 2 grey chairs D.R., re-enter R.1, set blue chair spike #6 C., exit R.1, re-enter R.1, set gold chair spike #6 R., exit R.1.

Cue light: Enter L.1, set tv spike #6, exit L.1.

Cue light: Enter R.1, strike blue chair R.1, re-enter R.1, strike gold chair R.1.

Cue light: Enter L.1, strike TV L.1.

Cue light: Enter D.R., cross U. through panels 1 and 2, set gold chair spike #7 C., exit L.1.

Cue light: Enter D.R., set blue chair spike #7 R., exit D.R.

Cue light: Enter D.L., set grey armchair and type-writer table spike #8, exit D.L.

Cue light: Enter D.R., strike empty gold chair L.1.

Cue light: Enter D.R., strike blue chair D.R.

Cue light: Enter D.L., set grey chair spike #9, exit D.L.

Cue light: Enter D.L., strike typewriter table D.L.

Cue light: Enter D.R., set park bench spike #10, exit D.R.

Cue light: Enter D.L., strike 2 grey chairs D.L.

COSTUME PLOT

EMILY STILSON
  Light-grey knit wool, bias-cut skirt
  Matching long-sleeved, collarless top
  Grey hose
  Grey, low-heeled pumps
  Grey knit-weave shawl
  Loose, bulky weave black, white, and grey-blue wool
    coat

AMY
  Light-tan, tailored blouse
  Light-brown, pleated wool tweed skirt (with blue and
    white accents)
  Brown, low-heeled working shoes
  White therapist's jacket
  Light-grey, tailored winter coat
  Loose-knit beige scarf

FIRST DOCTOR
  Light-grey pants
  Tailored pinstripe shirt
  Blue neck tie
  Black loafers
  Full-length, white doctor's coat

FIRST NURSE
  White nurse's uniform
  White hose
  White nurse's shoes
  Nurse's cap
  Grey cardigan sweater

SECOND DOCTOR
   Charcoal grey pants
   Tailored pinstripe shirt
   Blue, white and grey patterned neck tie
   Tan suede walking shoes
   Full-length, white doctor's coat

SECOND NURSE
   White nurse's uniform
   White hose
   White nurse's shoes
   Nurse's cap

BILLY
   Brown corduroy work trousers
   Red, brown and white plaid flannel shirt
   Brown work shoes

MR. BROWNSTEIN
   Grey pants
   Blue tailored, button-down oxford shirt
   Grey bow tie
   Black shoes
   Dark-grey cardigan

MRS. TIMMINS
   Light-olive wool skirt
   Matching cashmere, short-sleeved top
   Tan hose
   Tan mocassins

STAGE HAND/ORDERLY
   Soft-soled black shoes
   Black trousers
   Black open-necked shirt
   Long grey lab jacket

SOUND CUE SHEET

CUE:	DESCRIPTION
A	Ticking of mantle clock
B	Chaos
C	Hospital background; PA announcement
D	Window raising followed by birds chirping; fade hospital noise
E	All Stops
F	MS gagging
G	MS's voice, "Habst aporcshop . . ."
H	Door flapping, wind
I	Accelerated hospital background
J	Hospital noise stops
K	Voice over PA, "Mrs. Howard . . ."
L	Wind, accelerating, abrupt stop
M	Voices, and Hospital background
N	Reverberating tone, increasing intensity 39 secs
O	Door flapping, wind
P	Hospital background
Q	MS's voice, "Dark now again . . ."
R	Hospital background
S	Wind
T	Wind chimes, birds chirping
U	Fade birds down
V	Fade birds out
W	Door flapping, wind
X	Increase wind
Y	Fade out wind
Z	Wind, random chimes

CUE:	DESCRIPTION
AA	Ella Fitzgerald, "scat" singing
BB	Singing fades out

CC	Birds
DD	Fade out birds
EE	''Burke'' cue
FF	Doctor's voice ''on tape''
GG	Repeat FF
HH	Voice stops
II	Winter wind, airplane circling in distance
JJ	Fade wind down
KK	Wind fades up
LL	Increase wind
MM	Fade out Wind
NN	Deafening door flapping
OO	Musical tone, then random chimes

NEW BROADWAY DRAMAS
from
SAMUEL FRENCH, INC.

AMADEUS – AMERICAN BUFFALO – BENT –
COLD STORAGE – COME BACK TO THE 5 &
DIME, JIMMY DEAN, JIMMY DEAN –
COMEDIANS – THE CRUCIFER OF BLOOD –
THE CURSE OF AN ACHING HEART – DO YOU
TURN SOMERSAULTS? – THE DRESSER –
DUET FOR ONE – EMINENT DOMAIN – FAITH
HEALER – THE GIN GAME – HEARTLAND –
I WON'T DANCE – KNOCKOUT – A LESSON
FROM ALOES – NED AND JACK – NUTS –
PAST TENSE – SCENES AND REVELATIONS –
THE SHADOW BOX – THE SUICIDE –
TO GRANDMOTHER'S HOUSE WE GO –
THE WATER ENGINE – WINGS

For descriptions of plays, consult our free Basic Catalogue of Plays.

Other Publications for Your Interest

AGNES OF GOD

(LITTLE THEATRE—DRAMA)

By JOHN PIELMEIER

3 women—1 set (bare stage)

Doctor Martha Livingstone, a court-appointed psychiatrist, is asked to determine the sanity of a young nun accused of murdering her own baby. Mother Miriam Ruth, the nun's superior, seems bent on protecting Sister Agnes from the doctor, and Livingstone's suspicions are immediately aroused. In searching for solutions to various mysteries (who killed the baby? Who fathered the child?) Livingstone forces all three women, herself included, to face some harsh realities in their own lives, and to re-examine the meaning of faith and the commitment of love. "Riveting, powerful, electrifying new drama . . . three of the most magnificent performances you will see this year on any stage anywhere . . . the dialogue crackles."—Rex Reed, N.Y. Daily News. ". . . outstanding play . . . deals intelligently with questions of religion and psychology."—Mel Gussow, N.Y. Times. ". . . unquestionably blindingly theatrical . . . cleverly executed blood and guts evening in the theatre . . . three sensationally powered performances calculated to wring your withers."—Clive Barnes, N.Y. Post. (#236)

(For Future Release.
Royalty, $60-$40, when available.)
(Posters available)

COME BACK TO THE 5 & DIME, JIMMY DEAN, JIMMY DEAN

(ADVANCED GROUPS—DRAMA)

By ED GRACZYK

1 man, 8 women—Interior

In a small-town dime store in West Texas, the Disciples of James Dean gather for their twentieth reunion. Now a gaggle of middle-aged women, the Disciples were teenagers when Dean filmed "Giant" two decades ago in nearby Marfa. One of them, an extra in the film, has a child whom she says was conceived by Dean on the "Giant" set; the child is the Jimmy Dean of the title. The ladies' reminiscences mingle with flash-backs to their youth; then the arrival of a stunning and momentarily unrecognized woman sets off a series of confrontations that upset their self-deceptions and expose their well-hidden disappointments. "Full of homespun humor . . . surefire comic gems."—N.Y. Post. "Captures convincingly the atmosphere of the 1950s."—Women's Wear Daily. (#5147)

(Royalty, $60-$40.)

FAVORITE BROADWAY DRAMAS

from

SAMUEL FRENCH, INC.

ALL THE WAY HOME – THE AMEN CORNER –
AMERICAN BUFFALO – ANASTASIA – ANGEL
STREET – BECKET – THE BELLE OF AMHERST –
BUTLEY – COLD STORAGE – COME BACK, LITTLE
SHEBA – A DAY IN THE DEATH OF JOE EGG –
A DELICATE BALANCE – THE DESPERATE HOURS
– THE ELEPHANT MAN – EQUUS – FORTUNE AND
MEN'S EYES – A HATFUL OF RAIN – THE
HOMECOMING – J.B. – KENNEDY'S CHILDREN –
LOOK HOMEWARD, ANGEL – A MAN FOR ALL
SEASONS – THE MIRACLE WORKER – A MOON FOR
THE MISBEGOTTEN – NO PLACE TO BE SOMEBODY
– ONE FLEW OVER THE CUCKOO'S NEXT – OUR
TOWN – A RAISIN IN THE SUN – THE RIVER
NIGER – THE SHADOW BOX – SIX CHARACTERS
IN SEARCH OF AN AUTHOR – STICKS AND BONES –
THE SUBJECT WAS ROSES – TEA AND SYMPATHY –
THE VISIT – WINGS

For descriptions of all our plays, consult our Basic Catalogue of Plays – available FREE.